MARTIAL ARTS FUN

by Cari Meister

PEBBLE
a capstone imprint

Pebble Emerge is published by Pebble, an imprint of Capstone.
1710 Roe Crest Drive, North Mankato, Minnesota 56003
www.capstonepub.com

Library of Congress Cataloging-in-Publication Data
Names: Meister, Cari, author.
Title: Martial arts fun / by Cari Meister.
Description: North Mankato, Minnesota : Capstone Press, [2021] | Series: Sports fun | Includes bibliographical references and index. | Audience: Ages 6-8 | Audience: Grades 2-3 | Summary: "Martial Arts are thrilling to watch, but they're even more fun to do! Kids can take part in the sport by learning what martial arts are, what gear and skills are needed, what happens during lessons, and how to be a good sport. A skill-building activity helps kids participate in the fun"-- Provided by publisher.
Identifiers: LCCN 2020037716 (print) | LCCN 2020037717 (ebook) | ISBN 9781977132284 (hardcover) | ISBN 9781977154637 (pdf) | ISBN 9781977156297 (kindle edition)
Subjects: LCSH: Martial arts--Juvenile literature.
Classification: LCC GV1101.35 .M45 2021 (print) | LCC GV1101.35 (ebook) | DDC 796.8--dc23
LC record available at https://lccn.loc.gov/2020037716
LC ebook record available at https://lccn.loc.gov/2020037717

Image Credits
iStockphoto: FatCamera, 5, 19, Gerville, 21, OcusFocus, cover; Shutterstock: 7stock, 4, Dmytro Zinkevych, 12, 18, guruXOX, 6, 15, Happy Together, 9, hchjjl, back cover, 1, Iakov Filimonov, 11, 13, Microgen, 14, Nomad_Soul, 10, Satyrenko, 17, Serhii Bobyk, 7

Editorial Credits
Editor: Jill Kalz; Designer: Tracy McCabe; Media Researcher: Eric Gohl; Production Specialist: Katy LaVigne

All internet sites appearing in back matter were available and accurate when this book was sent to press.

TABLE OF CONTENTS

Words in **bold** are in the glossary.

WHAT ARE MARTIAL ARTS?

Two kids kick. They punch. They yell, "Heeyah!" What are they doing? They are doing martial arts!

Martial arts are sets of skills. They help people **protect** themselves. They can also be used for fighting. Today, many people do martial arts as a fun sport.

There are many kinds of martial arts. Each kind has different skills. **Karate**, **kung fu**, and **tae kwon do** are a few kinds of martial arts. **Judo** and **jujitsu** are too. All of them help make a person feel good. They make the body and mind strong.

WHAT DO I NEED?

You need a uniform to do martial arts. It has a top and a bottom. The top is a long-sleeved jacket. The bottom is long pants. The uniform is loose so you can move easily. It is often white. But it can be blue or black. You also need a white belt.

WHERE DO I LEARN?

You learn to do martial arts in a studio. Studios are big, open spaces. There is lots of room to kick and punch. Soft floor mats protect your body when you fall.

The walls may have large mirrors. Seeing
how your body moves helps you learn.

HOW DO I LEARN?

Before you do martial arts, you stretch. Stretching gets you warmed up. It keeps your body loose. Next, you learn how to move the right way.

You kick and punch. You spin, jump, and **block**. You also learn how to calm your mind and think clearly. You learn how to deal with bad feelings in a good way.

Once you know the moves, you **spar**. Sparring is like practice fighting. Most of the time, you spar with your classmates. You may also spar with your **master**.

Everyone starts with a white belt. In time, you can test for a different color. If you don't pass your test, that's OK. You can practice more. Then you can take the test again.

HOW CAN I BE A GOOD SPORT?

Martial arts are most fun when everyone is a good sport. Go to class with a smile. Watch and listen to your master. Practice each skill until it's the best it can be. Ask for help when you need it. And be thankful when you get that help.

Be kind to your classmates. Be willing to help them if they need it. Do your best and be fair. If you lose, don't get upset. Learn from the loss and keep trying.

It can take a long time to do martial arts well. Don't give up. You can do it!

SKILL BUILDER: GO THE DISTANCE

Try these exercises at home. Stick with them, and you should have more energy to punch, kick, and block through any class. Practice in front of a mirror to make sure you are doing your skills the right way.

- Pick one thing to practice, such as kicks or punches. Time yourself doing it 10 times. Do three sets of 10 every day. After two weeks, time yourself again. Are you faster or slower?

- See how many times you can do one skill, such as a kick or punch. How many can you do before your body can't do any more? Write down the number. Repeat this exercise every other day for two weeks. Did your number go up or down?

GLOSSARY

block (BLAHK)—to make a move with your body to keep from getting hit

judo (JOO-doh)—a martial art from Japan that grew out of jujitsu

jujitsu (joo-JIT-soo)—a martial art from Japan; the name means "gentle art"

karate (kuh-RAH-tee)—a martial art from Japan; the name means "empty hand"

kung fu (KUNG FOO)—a set of martial arts from China

master (MA-stur)—a teacher of martial arts who has practiced it a long time

protect (proh-TEKT)—to keep safe

spar (SPAR)—to practice fight

tae kwon do (TY KWON DOH)—a martial art from Korea

READ MORE

Brainard, Jason. *Brazilian Jujitsu*. New York: PowerKids Press, 2020.

Faust, Daniel R. *Kung Fu*. New York: PowerKids Press, 2020.

Shaffer, Jody Jensen. *Who Is Jackie Chan?* New York: Penguin Workshop, 2020.

INTERNET SITES

Martial Arts Facts for Kids
https://kids.kiddle.co/Martial_arts

Taekwondo Facts
http://www.softschools.com/facts/sports/taekwondo_facts/794/

INDEX